In the heat of the summer

Sara Jones

BookLeaf Publishing

Presentation by *BookLeaf Publishing*

Web: www.bookleafpub.com

E-mail: info@bookleafpub.com

ISBN: 9789357743884

First edition 2023

To S. F.

The first time I saw you

You were about four and a half feet tall
 You were reserved
 You wore sweatshirts
 Thinking back, it was probably hiding your
scars
 Thinking back, I probably messed it up by
asking you how you are.

Are you okay?
Okay, it is not a thing people can be
It's a word we use
When we don't understand
what we see
Okay and good and fine
It's not saying
All the things that we hide

You said you sleep little at night
I thought that's why you were always so high
You spoke about death
And cars breaking your bones
You had numbers
Of how many people die each year
Looking back, You weren't even scared
You said it like a story

You'd read to your kid sister
In a vioce that makes you sleepy
And helps you dream of cotton candy.

You told my your name
It rolled of your tongue
Like you'd punch it
So rough it could cut
And it hurt
Because i have done that
And I've been there

The signs I didn't see

The sweatshirts pulled down to your wrist
Even in 90 degrees
The fact that you never ate
Never laughed
You spoke about death
Like it was your long- lost friend
Your eyes barely open
You were never fully awake
The mono syllables you spoke in
The way everything triggered you
And made you freak out
The time you told me that you swallowed pills
in front of your dad
He did nothing? I asked
You said he questioned you if you were
pregnant or depressed
And you laughed
And he walked away
And that was that
Dad's don't do that. I wanted to yell
Instead, I drank coffee
And thought everything was swell

The times we were maybe, a little bit happy

We weren't always morbid
Sometimes, we were actually fine
We cracked jokes
And ate ice cream in cones

Sometimes i could see light in your brown eyes
Sometimes your smile was so freaking bright.

I shared my moms brownie
I told you I hate dressing up
And that wearing something other than a t-shirt
and jeans
To visit my family
Was corrupt

Sometimes we spoke about the songs that we
loved
Got stuck on a lryic we couldn't remember
It made us go insane
But we laughed about it anyway

Your brown eyes were orange
Like a beautiful dancing ember

See Sometimes you were happy
Sometimes I was too
Maybe in the moments that you forgot the scars
And let yourself breathe
But I doubt it was even real

The first day you don't show
up

You were supposed to come
But never showed
I sat there waiting
Hoping you were only late
Hoping you were okay
And fine
And good
And all the words we vowed never to use

I didn't see you for the next week

Psychward

I know you're there
 I can hear it in your voice
I am on the stree
 As I clutch the phone
I'm a sweating
It's in the heat of the summer
Yet my heart feels like october
Like I am stuck in an avalanche
Drifting away
With the snow
With the wind
With the sea
I am fine
You say
They have paper spoons
The food is mushy like applesauce
I don't have to see my family
 And I have my own guardian angel that watches
me pee
 Guess what they even have a TV

The day that my heart breaks

I was once there
Not in the psychward
But a step before
It really wasn't that long ago

A heart is supposed to beat through the hard shit
in life
It's supposed to stay strong
Yet I cry

I should have
Would have
Could have
It replays in my mind
All the days I spent with you
Where did things go wrong

Fuck
Fuck
Fuck
My heart is going to give out
It was never that strong
It has been broken before
It's going to happen again

If only
What if
Maybe
But
Please

So many words unsaid
So many things I could have done

My heart failed me
Yours won

The part where I convince myself that I am fine

Fine
I think I am fine
You were just a friend
Now you're miles away
Crazy and hurting
Practically gone

I am fine
I don't need to see you everyday
I have got a family
Mom
Who bakes a killer apple pie
Dad
Who is teaching me how to drive
Drive...I don't want to drive
What if I crash into the wall
Because I have had enough of this life
Fuck.
Stop it...
You. are. fine.
You have sisters who love you
A brother that loves annoying you
A boss
And a friend

And a class
And your pens
And paper
And drawings
And writings
You are fine
You are more than fine
You are not her
You're not going to die
You are fine
Everything is alright
Lair liar liar
Iie

1 mother duck

I have lost things
 I have lost my homework assignment in the
seventh grade
 My shoes when I was five
I lost dad's Dad before I was even here
I was losing stuff forever
Practically since birth

 There is a nursery rhyme
 Where a mother duck and 8 of her ducklings
stand at the foot of a hill
 And every five minutes or so
 A baby duck
Goes over the hill
And far away
8
7
6
5
4
3
2
1
0
The mother duck is all alone

None of her ducklings are coming home

The nursery rhyme ends with all the ducklings
running down the hill
In a hurry
To thier mommy

I am the mother duck of the story
Losing and losing
So much losing that it's getting gory

But unlike the ending in the rhyme
I don't think I am getting back the things that
have gone
Not now
Not today
Not this time

How summer is for everyone else

Dad
He cleans the garage
Barbecues every night
He buys a Ford pickup truck
And goes driving on the dirt road

Mom
Plants a garden of yellow white and pink
Tends to her vegetable patch
Makes fruit soup
And salad
Tries to make homemade yogurt
Goes to the beach with Dad and the kids
Do you want to come honey
She asks me
No thank you
Sorry

Rachel
Hangs with her friends at the mall. Goes
swimming. Tries wearing makeup for the first
time and over does the glitter
'you can never over do glitter, silly'

Juliet
Practices her guitar and paints her room purple,
goes to sleep away camp for two weeks, comes
back burned from the sun

Jack
Rides his bike
Rides his bike
Rides his bike
Rides his bike
Rides his bike
Rides his bike
Rides his bike
Rides his bike
Falls of his bike

One night on the road

I stand on the road
Crying
Tears like a flood
I am waiting for a car to come
run me over
So I die
I wait and wait
But its late
No one is driving
I cry
More
Cry
Cry
Cry
Fuck
Shit
Why can't I die

Mom

I wake up the next day
It feels funny
Waking up on a normal day
The morning after standing on the road
Wishing it all away

Mom makes pancakes for breakfast
Mom does her yoga
Mom drinks her coffee
Mom
I say
I stood on the road yesterday
but no cars came
Mom says
what the hell
What were you thinking
You could have died
Jesus mom
That was it
That was the plan
Die

She cries

Die

Die
Die
Does the word bother you
And hurt your ears
Die
Die
Die
I wanted to die

I miss you I hate you

I miss seeing your face
 Hearing your vioce
 I miss seeing your smile
 And your eyes
 I miss the way you ate my moms brownie like
you have never tasted brownie before
 I miss you
 And the things we would do
 I miss discussing how much fun dying would be
 Becuase everything was better when you were
with me

 I hate you because I am still here
 Thanks to you almost killing yourself
 I hate you because when I tell mom and dad and
Rachel and juliet about you
 They cry
 I hate you because you are making it hard to
live
 I hate you for almost dying
 I hate you for not thinking of me
 Most of all, I hate you...
 I hate you because it hurts to miss you

Summer ends

It's weird
I barely knew you for two weeks
Now, two months later
I still think of you

You and you and only you
And I am sick of thinking about you
And the fact that you don't pick up when I call
And I don't know if you are alive

You in all those sweatshirts that made me sweat
You laying at the foot of my bed
You and you and you
Only you

Please come the fuck back

Glitter

There is a song called Glitter
By Patric Dempsey
It talks about the fact that grief
Is something you can't brush off
And get rid of

But glitter sparkles
And glitter is nice
Glitter makes people laugh
Grief is not glitter

I remember when I was five
We went to the beach
Feeling so alive

We played on the sun
In the water
In the sand
When we came back home
Tried to get the sand off
Nothing worked

I had sand in my hair
Ears
In between my toes

I had sand in me for the next week
My mouth
Hands
Nose

Grief is like sand
It doesn't sparkle or shine
It's just there
Itching. Like crazy
Constantly reminding you that it is not going
away

Trigger

A match
A flame
A mistake
Shame
A cause
Effect
A rock against a window
A Crack
Betrayal
It hurts
A burn
It burns
It's a trigger
And its outcome
Like pull a gun
And a bullet
Like forgetting an anniversary
And a pile of laundry
A trigger
And it's outcome
Like you trying to take your life
And me trying to take mine

I am sorry

I am sorry
How many times can you say
I am sorry
I am sorry
I am sorry
I really am
Today

I'm sorry mom saw the blood
And the cracks
And the bottle
And the pain

I am sorry dad had to call for an ambulance
I am sorry Jack awoke
I am sorry for juliet friends that were on the
phone when she yelled

I am sorry for rachel and her missing all the fun

I am sorry
In all honesty
I am sorry
I am sorry
I am sorry

Mom dad
I am sorry

I am so freaking sorry that it didn't work
That I am not dead

Winter summer fall spring

It's fall now
 Am I still going to think of you in the winter
 When it snows
 Rains
 And pours
 When the cold seeps into my bones

 Am I going to think of you in the spring
 When the sky clears
 And it's baby blue
 When flowers bloom
 And the grass is green
 When the wind seeps in my clothes

 Ami giong to think of you when I look up at the
stars at night
 Wonder if you see the same wonderful light

 And how about next summer
 Am i going to pencil in the date
 In a freak calander
 Celebrate it with a cream cake
 And candles
 And confetti
 Am I going to say

July 22nd
The day you tried to die
Am I going to dance
And sing
Like it's a birthday

Maybe
Just maybe
Do you think
Maybe I need...

Help

Help
It's the bravest thing I have ever said
I need help
Desperately
Sorely
Really
Badly
I need help

I have got a mom and a dad
And two sisters
And a brother
I got a life
One, only one life

And sometimes I want to die

Help me
Please
I don't want to drown
In these moments
I need someone to hold my hand
Help me
Help me
Please help me

Teach me to breathe
Teach me that I am okay
Teach me to live
Again
Help
Help
Help
Help me
Desperately
Sorely
Really
Badly

Are you okay? mom asks
I nod
And I think of you, I hope you're fine

If you want to know
What's up with me
I am good
Can't you see